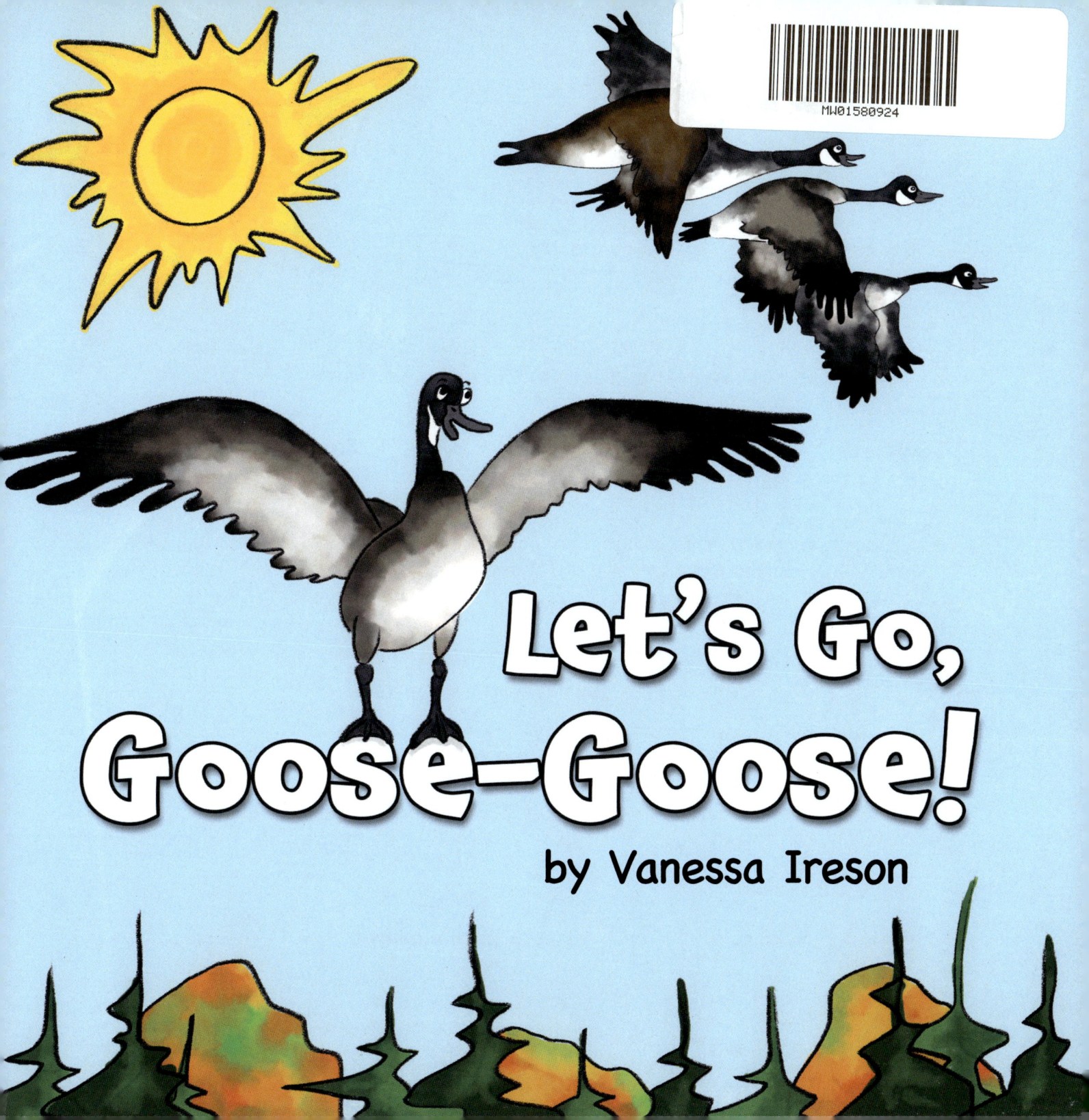

Copyright ©2022 Vanessa Ireson

Written and Illustrated by Vanessa Ireson

Published by Miriam Laundry Publishing Company

miriamlaundry.com

All rights reserved. This book or any portion thereof may not be reproduced or used in any manner whatsoever without the express written permission from the author except for the use of brief quotations in a book review.

PB ISBN 978-1-990107-77-1

e-Book ISBN 978-1-990107-78-8

FIRST EDITION

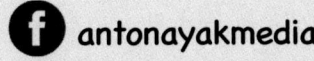 antonayakmedia 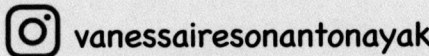 vanessairesonantonayak  antonayak

For David and Stephen,
who introduced the real Goose-Goose to
my imagination and who inspire me every day.

And for Mom and Dad,
Thank you. For everything.

In a colourful forest by a shimmering lake, a chattering squirrel gives a pine branch a shake.

A pinecone streaks down and lands with a thump, scattering the seeds of a startled chipmunk.

Red maple leaves flutter down from the trees, and high in the blue, soar the geese in their vees.

"HONK! HONK! HONK!" Canada Geese call.
BRRRR ... the air's getting cold! Welcome to fall!

A boy and his dog explore the lakeshore.
He fetches flat rocks, at least three or four.

He avoids grabbing one, just in time. Phew!
That's not a pebble! It's a piece of goose poo!

With a flick of the wrist, he makes the rocks skip.
He counts the ripples. Jump! Bounce! Flip!

Hey! That last splash wasn't his stone...
There's something moving out there all alone!

What's that in the lake? A log or a rock?
Could that be a goose, away from its flock?

A white, feathered butt sticks up in the air.

Yup, it's a goose slurping seaweed down there.

Up pops a head, with a beak full of slime.
Its eyes open wide, and it moves just in time!

"Coming in hot! Duck, Goose-Goose!"
Gracy splashes down, knocking feathers loose.

"Not your thing?! Not an option!"
Gracy squawks, aghast.

"Look! Frosty leaves! Icy lake!
Launch time's coming fast!"

A mean goose named Gary and his friends swim by.
"Don't waste your time, Gracy. *Goof-Goof* can't fly.
I think he's a chicken! Bock! Bock! Bock!
Have you ever seen him fly? Or can he only walk?"

Angry geese flap and hiss, and Goose-Goose is mad!
He wags his wings in Gary's face. Oh, this is looking bad.

"Gary Goose, leave him alone!
He'll fly when he's ready!"

"I **CAN** fly!" And off he goes! Starting slow but steady!

He loop-d-loops!

He flips and spins!

He dive-bombs from up high!

Gracy grins, sticks out her tongue and joins him in the sky.

They glide together, wings in sync. Gracy takes the lead. Honking to encourage him, they start to pick up speed.

"So, why do you never train with us? Don't you like to fly?"

"What if I don't want to fly south?" asks Goose-Goose, feeling shy.

"What else would you do in winter?!" Gracy cries in shock.

A startled goose in a vee nearby, swerves.

Bump! "Squawk!"

"Shhhh!" He hisses, turning red.
"I like the home we've got.
The lake, the beach, the boy, his dog.
And our favourite rock!"

Goose-Goose and Gracy catch a draft of wind and start to soar.
"What if there are no trees down south? Or a stony shore?"

"Oh Goose-Goose, that's just silly. Why would there be no trees?"

"They say there are, but how do we know? Do we just wait and see?
Everything will be different! And scary ... and new."

"Well, I'm excited. And curious. But a little nervous, too."

They fly along in silence. Goose-Goose looks down and gasps. "Uh oh, Gracy. Something's wrong! Where are we?" he asks.

The sky is empty. The lake is gone. A playground is below. Out of breath and scared, they land. This is strange. Oh, no!

"Yikes, Goose-Goose! I think we're lost! Whatever will we do?" But Goose-Goose is wonderstruck. He marvels at the view.

A kid slips down a shiny slide. A merry-go-round spins. With gleaming eyes, Goose-Goose cries, "Let's go try the swings!"

They play tag with a little girl and learn to play hopscotch.

A crowd cheers for a soccer team.
They snack on grass and watch.

Goose-Goose grins. "This is fun! New is pretty great!"
Gracy nods and laughs along. They stay until it's late.

It's time for them to head on back, but which way should they go?
Maybe if he'd gone to class, then Goose-Goose might know.

"We're supposed to learn to navigate. But they haven't taught that yet.
Oh, why did we stray this far?" Gracy starts to fret.

Deep down, Goose-Goose has a hunch that he can work it out.
His goosey brain is built to know, he feels without a doubt.

"Then I think we go THIS way." They rise above the trees.
It's like a magnet's pulling him. "C'mon! Follow me!"

They head toward the setting sun, almost side by side.
They form their own half of a vee, which helps them zoom and glide.

All of a sudden, Goose-Goose points. "Hey, I see our lake!"
"There's the beach! And our rock!" The geese put on the brakes.

"There you are! You made it safe!" The flock honks happily.
Even Gary's glad they're back — one big family.

They land on their rock and share a hug to Gracy's "Home sweet home!"
"For now," says Goose-Goose with a smile, "I'm not afraid to roam."

The next few days are a blur as Goose-Goose gets up to speed. Practicing vees with your team can be fun indeed!

Soon they wake to fluffy snow that frosts the beach and trees. Water ripples. Geese take off. The sky is full of vees.

Goose-Goose and Gracy shout with glee,
"Let's do this! Today's the day!"
The boy with the dog waves farewell.
The geese honk and fly away.

Goose-Goose Facts

- I'm a real goose! I live in a forest in Ontario, Canada!
- Writer/illustrator Vanessa Ireson and her family, David, Steve and Daisy the Dog, are my neighbours! I love it when they visit me.
- David gave me my name: Goose-Goose!
- Gracy is my best friend. Geese are very loyal and pair up for life. We can live up to 20 years.
- We eat plants, grass, berries, seeds and nuts. (It's best not to try to feed us.)
- A group of geese on the ground is called a gaggle! In the air we're called a skein or a team.
- Baby geese are called goslings. They are born in the spring and are ready to fly in the fall.
- We migrate to warmer homes for the winter and return to where we were born in spring. We can travel hundreds of kilometers.
- We use our good memory and the earth's magnetic field to find our way, like a built-in GPS!
- We fly in v-formations because if we work together, we can go farther, faster and look out for each other. We take turns being the leader!
- We hiss, honk and flap our wings when we're protecting our territory. Just back away slowly, stay calm and try not to step in goose poop!
- Geese poop 100 times a day!
- Vanessa loves to be creative and tell stories with words and images. She has taken a gazillion photos of me and my flock. You might see some of them on her Instagram page: @vanessairesonantonayak

Manufactured by Amazon.ca
Bolton, ON